KIM HOFFMAN

RELAX, RELEASE, REBOOT

MY KEY TO UNLOCK UNDETECTED DEPRESSION

RELAX, RELEASE, REBOOT
Copyright © 2024 Kim Hoffman.

Script Marker
500 8th Avenue FRNT 3 #1560
Manhattan, NY 10018
516-684-9243
www.Script-Marker.com

Because of the dynamic nature of the Internet, any web addresses or links contained in this book may have changed since publication and may no longer be valid. The views expressed in the work are solely those of the author and do not necessarily reflect the views of the publisher, and the publisher hereby disclaims any responsibility for them.

ISBN 9979-8-89523-018-3 (Paperback)
ISBN 979-8-89523-019-0 (Ebook)

Printed in the United States of America.

TO THOSE LIKE myself who refused to believe that depression can show itself with many and often different moods and actions in one's life; that it will, without a doubt, cause so many reactions from it as well; and to all those who refuse to admit they need help with it, you are truly missing out on a better life.

If you're suffering with depression but not sure how to ask for help, just remember that you're not "crazy." Look at it this way: Technology of devices such as computers and cell phones can help us communicate with a lot of the world until they need help from an overloaded meltdown too, and we all know to shut them down for a while to reboot until they function on their own again.

So please take it from me, a very stubborn German computer born in Speedy Creek, Saskatchewan, Canada, that if I can ask for help, then there is help for you too. Remember to *relax, release,* and *reboot* because without your brain, you cannot walk; without your brain, you cannot feel; without your brain, you cannot talk; and without your brain, you cannot heal.

So please, you do matter, and never let these next two words scare you like they did me. It's only two words, and you can learn to enjoy life again: mental health.

My name is Kim Hoffman, and this is my life's struggle with undetected depression.

I was one boy out of six, plus one baby sister who brought seventh heaven because she was the last born, and wouldn't you know it? She was born on Dad's birthday, October 20, so fitting seeing that they tried for a girl in the first place. I fit in the middle of the boys all within a year of each other. My oldest brother had a disability, and I'm sure we learned true compassion from him. To say Mom and Dad had their hands full was the truest understatement you could think of.

We came to Moose Jaw from Swift Current or "Speedy Creek," as most refer it to when I was around four years old. Dad bought our first house here, still with outdoor facilities that seemed to be a block away to a little guy when you had to go out at night. But I was glad they were outside as the neighbor kids fed me dog biscuits throughout the day and said they were cookies, But enough about our beautifully situated outhouse and treats.

The house was bigger and better than the shack we lived in before. At least we had two bedrooms that could be used here. Let me explain. Dad was a motorcycle cop in Speedy Creek until his accident. He flew off his motorcycle when a car cut him off, he landed on his back and broke it. They operated on it, but these were hillbilly surgeons compared to those of today, and the career he loved was over. He was well enough to take on other jobs for a number of years but was never really happy. That was when, I believe, his teachings of depression 101 started.

With not a lot of money coming in, we moved out to a house/shack just outside of Swift, where we had a two bedroom house. We soon learned we could only use oneof them; one was infested with mice so bad it had to be boarded shut. That meant five of us boys shared the one bedroom with mom and dad while my eldest brother slept in the living room on the sofa. That's why now I hate mice.

Now we are living in a little house in Moose Jaw full of boys and outdoor facilities when a baby sister pops into our lives, as I mentioned before, on Dad's birthday. This house was no place for a newborn, but we lived there for a bit longer until Dad could afford a larger home.

It was in this house that I have my first memories of seeing Dad drinking after work. He was drinking with a native fellow from across the alley when things started to heat up, and the terror began when the man grabbed a kitchen knife. They fought and rolled around as we were all screaming and crying as loud as we could. Dad eventually did get control and knocked him out and then sat on him till police arrived. That was the first but not the last scar embedded with more to come.

We moved to a larger, beautiful home with four bedrooms, a big fireplace that became a centerpiece for family pictures, and I believe, our first TV. But it wasn't long before I started hearing and seeing things again. Lots of memories are still locked away and might not surface because they have been hidden for far too long. We lived there for the next four years or so.

With a new school, lots of friends and playing as a child should have given me happy memories. That's why I buried memories like these ones: Dad coming in the side door so drunk he fell downstairs backward onto a water meter. Again something that could have finished him off. There is another random memory of him rinsing his mouth with aftershave before leaving to work to cover the booze on his breath. There are memories of Mom getting a phone call that Dad had driven into a pole.

Yes, like I said, there are good memories too, but as a kid, these visions are how we learn. I know they weren't done as punishment but were just mistakes in life. They loved us all I'm sure, even though I can't remember those words; they continued the best way they knew how. We were sent to Sunday school as others did back then to learn the words that our parents may have forgotten over the years. As I now know, some memories are just overlooked and some just find a dark place to hide.

We moved again to a smaller house that was nice; it had a garage with a ladder and an opening for up top that we used to house the pigeons we caught and raised that was so cool. We spent a lot of time up there, and I remember jumping out of there into big snow mounds below. It was this home where I saw more than my brothers did. Looking back, I know it must have been hard and stressful on my parents with one income. Mom couldn't work with a child with a disability and the rest of us, but did they have to disagree on everything all the time?

I do remember a lot of great times: my brothers and I playing as friends because we were all a year apart, with six years between the youngest and the eldest. We all hung out with each other's friends. It didn't matter when you're playing football, basketball, or baseball together—that part was always fun.

It was an escape without knowing it. The other side was when I developed asthma and could no longer sleep in the basement because of the mildew. I had to sleep upstairs, and that's where I heard and saw the things that went on that the others didn't see. Let's just say I was there to see firsthand what they only heard. By the time they ran upstairs, they had already missed what I had seen and heard, and I just continued to see more and more.

It's not fun to jump in between the two people you love the most in the world having a battle for control when Dad stumbles in at 2:00 a.m. This went on for years. I would push him away from Mom, almost daring him to hit me, and one time he did. Without knowing it then, my life was about to take a big turn.

As a twelve year old, I didn't have a fully developed mind to deal with what I was seeing and hearing. I decided to ask my brothers to help but got nowhere after telling them what I saw and how I felt. They would say he's not that bad or he just had too much and he will be fine tomorrow. Maybe they just forgot about all the times we had to go to our neighbor's house at 2:00 and 3:00 a.m., or maybe "they were just planned sleepovers ya, that's it."

My youngest brother, a close friend, and I used to catch pigeons on the Manitoba Street bridge overlooking the river and dam at least once a week, and we had mastered scaling every inch of it. I remember one time, a train was coming as we were about halfway across.

We had three options: run to the other end, but the ties were about eight inches apart and you had to skip over two or so just to to get up enough speed, but if you miss one, you're done—train 1, kid 0. Option two, you could climb down by scaling the sides, or option three, just jump off. Well, we all scattered and were able to laugh about it later.

Some time goes with little to no change at home. I again confronted Dad on his actions, and frankly, I can't remember why, but I remember he said that's it and knocked me from one side of a seven-foot sofa clear to the other side. I decided to get out; I'd had enough. Crying, I took off and ran past the hospital up the trail and I climbed the bridge by myself for the first time. I waited and waited for that train to come, but there wasn't one that day. I looked down at the concrete dam; I jumped off leaping toward it. I remember it being scary and peaceful at the same time. I missed my target, and I hit the water very hard. I came up and grabbed the concrete wall, as the water wanted to take me down.

I made it to Manitoba Street and wondered, *Why am I still here?* It was divine intervention, not that it would have meant anything to me at twelve or thirteen anyway, but looking back, I'm sure that this was the beginning of me locking up emotional memories and burying them deep within and where I lost my "key" to them all.

Now I was wet, cold, and hungry, but I stayed away from home until I dried off so they wouldn't question me. I can't remember hearing sorry from Dad either.

I missed a lot of school, or I just got tired. I know if Mom had a safe place to take us, she would have, as I've seen her so scared with me being always first on the scene and with no help/shelters as that of today. She was stuck, ultimately enabling him to continue; they only had the one income, so what could she do with seven children and be scared?

The drinking continued as did the verbal and emotional abuses with a dose of belt buckle for good measure. I saw Dad so angry he sent a jackknife flying at my older brother, it bounced once and stuck in his heel. I remember blood instantly coming into the picture, and the screaming started.

A few days would go by and he'd be drunk but wanted to say sorry by giving us money or candy, or taking us fishing. Fishing was just an excuse to get drunk with a fishing rod, but it still was better than the yelling. One time, coming back from Long Lake, we were driving down the causeway and nearing the bottom curve when he went off the shoulder into the grass, with me screaming "Dad!" When he finally realized he cranked the wheel back to the road hard enough that our dog was inches from flying out the window, and with seat belts, we were flung around pretty good too. I know you're asking yourself, *Was I drunk?* I would have to say then and now, "Yup."

Another memory that terrified me was of him driving drunk down a one way street. The problem came when we met two cars coming up the same one way street head on. Once again, we went flying around as Dad drove over a curb and a walkway to get to the proper one way street, with tires squealing and the car scraping the bottom. He traded that car off for another shortly after.

If that sounds like a recipe you've ever heard before, just know it's not normal, as I came to believe it was. There was so much denial and hiding the truth that by age fifteen it really was becoming second nature. By jumping into the middle of their arguments for so long, it started giving me some power or control to jump in the middle of anyone's fight or disagreements to be the mediator and ultimately to control the situation.

I kept telling myself, I won't do things like my father did, but it was already too late for me. A good guy with a sense of humor and protecting nature could find out how to get things done by being controlling with aggression. It has replaced the depression in my life as I'm just now realizing it. I became driven to succeed in anything I took on like in my drawings or woodworking skills to where I wanted total "perfection." I believed that's what I needed to keep the "feelings" hidden that led up to the "bridge to water" attempt (depression) from returning again.

Now I was fighting for a better life, although the family had little to offer. I wanted more but was unsure how or even how to plan to get what it was I needed at fifteen. I wanted out and away so bad, but it wasn't possible at the time. I continued school and soon had my license to cruise. Finally, some independence, and with that I needed a job. I helped out my dad at his used furniture store, where I got to drive a very nice 1971 Chevy truck, which I burned the tires off every chance I could. I did work by picking up and delivering items, going to auctions, and bidding on what I thought would sell quickly. I taught myself to fix washers, dryers, clocks, radios, and TVs and to restore antiques. I continued this for about two more years until Dad's hard lifestyle caught up to him. He ended up in surgery for severe stomach pain. He went from 270 to 160 lb. I had never seen him look that way, and I thought his time was up.

I dropped out of school just before my seventeenth birthday to help with the store. Now I had a nice two door 1964 Ford Fairlane to cruise in and some money to party with, but it was never enough. Dad sold the store but continued to drink, just in lesser amounts. I started my first steam cleaning business at seventeen with the help of my uncle and another fellow who took me into the business world. They schooled me on cleaning (furniture, carpets, and drapery) and advertising. I'm a quick study and soon was making more than Dad in a month. I was in heaven, making up to $2,000 per week and nobody to spend it on but me and my friends.

My uncle liked his drinks too, but Dad drank hard stuff while his brother, my uncle, loved his wine and his stinky cigarettes he called them his "herbal medicine." Within a month, I tried a glass of Black Tower and a stinky cigarette while listening with my uncle to Boston on my new top of the line Techniques sound system, laughing till we cried. It was different with my uncle because he laughed with me or at me, and for the first time, drinking took bad memories of Dad's drinking and hid them away.

I had a blast spending money when coming back to my friends back home, partying nonstop at the lake for the next two summers. I took everything that I learned at home and started going to bars, convincing myself I only go to play pool!

I never started a fight but I seemed to end one almost every time I stayed for the last call. I remember taking winnings from four fellows after playing pool for over five hours. But when I walked out the back door, they decided they wanted their money back, and calling me a shark, they pushed me down the three steps, with my chin hitting the gravel, causing a good gash. I looked at the big mouth flapping his lips and put my foot in it, backhanding the guy to my right. The other two backed off because there were two officers across the street watching and waiting to see if I got into trouble. With two down and two to go, the officers came over and asked if I wanted to press charges. I said, "Not unless they do," and all four in perfect harmony said, "No, sir."

My dad used to tell stories of him on a train with a prisoner or two in the 1950s when he was an officer and the aggressive stories I always liked as a small fry. I guess it was his way of saying he could take care and protect us. So you see, I'm like him in many ways, so people say, although I never believed that until much later in life. I met and married the woman of any man's dream. She took me away from my past lifestyle and loved my humor, heart, and "body."

I met her at a cabaret where she pinched my butt, and it was love at first grab for sure. We married June 15, 1985, and had our first child March 27, 1986, just two days short of my wife's birthday. Now I had all my beautiful queen and princess at my side. I had the family I longed for, but could I be a better father?

Shortly after she was born, we moved to Estevan, Saskatchewan, where I took a branch manager's position, training direct sales to a staff of eight. It was a big responsibility at twenty four years of age. It was okay for a while, but it was hard when you're trying to keep a cranky secretary, a service writer with a no care attitude, as well as a sales staff upbeat and excited to want to be there. But nobody wanted to pump me up. The sales team, with the volume of sales they achieved, would simply keep them happy. But at the end of each month for several months, there was inventory missing, and it came all down on my shoulders to find the culprit taking my money. Now I'm drinking to hide the fact that I don't want to catch who it was because we've all become close, I thought.

I had my suspicions of which one it was. I placed an ad to service faulty products, listing off the model numbers that were missing, and people brought them in because they were new and the service repair was free. I recovered all but one unit and found one person who sold them all, and he wasn't even part of the sales team. It hurts to be stabbed deep. My drinking worsened after letting him go, and I filled his position with myself. The stress coupled with childhood depression grew from trying to be more than one man could be.

I was a perfectionist who was failing at something. I started taking my team on the road to different places to sell, but it really was an escape for me to drink after I pumped them up and sent them off. The fact that I was always fun and fair with my staff and yet having someone steal from me gave me the right amount of "poor me" to justify my drinking and by taking it home, where I could act on my subconscious, as that behavior was burned deep, and burns do leave ugly scars. All it did was hurt my wife emotionally to the point where I had to quit my job, and we moved back home to my next job that was waiting for me.

When you don't know why you're really up one day then you're so far down the next, it's the time to ask for help to figure it out early or you'll continue as I to master what I now know as denial.

Our home life changed. I became protective to the point of confinement so I wouldn't lose what was keeping me alive. We did everything together. One of us drove our daughter to school and picked her up, and if we couldn't, then my father in law would, even though we lived three blocks away. This continued for several more years. With every spare minute for the next three years, my daughter and I grew closer. On the golf course was where we would laugh, tell stories, and meet friends of mine who grew to love her too. We never did keep score, but we always kept those memories. Those moments healed my inner scars without knowing it then, and that meant I didn't need liquid suppression much those days. I must confess now that I took her away from her mother a lot of the time, but when we got back from our days together, she would always tell her mom how much fun we had in whatever we did.

It was 1993, and for achieving yet another sales goal, I won a trip for two to Mexico for seven days. We never had a honeymoon or a holiday since getting married; it was perfect timing. We left here at minus 28 and landed in Mexico at plus 34 at six thirty in the morning. Not being out of the country since a teen was awe inspiring. We proceeded to have a great time four out of the seven days because I burnt so freaking badly the first day that I couldn't stand, let alone walk for the next two of them. Not funny! Stop laughing already and keep reading until it gets better.

I wanted to pick up thirty large five dollar peso medallions for the customers it took to win this trip, but I only counted fifteen. I asked if he had more, and he said no but turned and asked how many I wanted. I replied thirty as long as they were like these. He says "Oh, my brother has some. Come, follow me," he said as he locked his shop. "Where are we going?" should have come out of my mouth, but being from Canada, it will be okay. We were trying to keep up to him, going down one alleyway and then through market after market, down another alley, and finally ending up in the market where his brother's shop was. Now we couldn't find our way back if we tried.

The shop was closed. As he reached in his pocket, I was really thinking now, but he just pulled out more keys. I know, I thought about guns or knives too! He unlocked the store, opened a drawer, and set a locked box on the counter, opened it, and showed me more medallions as he counted out fifteen more. I didn't even want to haggle with him because he still had to get us out of there. You see, all this time, he was almost running through stores, and it could have looked as if we were chasing him, but all I could think of was how I would knock him out if he decided to rob us. I swear "Stupid Canadians" was written on our backs with all the looks we got, but looking back on it now, he was in control not me, and now I know the feelings of my childhood again.

It's a nice place to visit, but watch out for the sun or you might fry your judgment too.

We returned to our jobs, with lots of snow and cold. It was back to work as usual for the next month and a half. That was until we found out we were pregnant again, and this time, we were having a "foreign baby." I mean this one was truly made in Mexico. When we told our daughter, she danced and jumped around the house for days, saying, "I always wanted a little sister." We had to ask her, "What if your sister is a brother?" She replied quickly, saying, "Girls can't be boys, Dad." She always makes my day better.

And seven and a half months later, she had her baby sister, born two days before my birthday. How cool because as I mentioned earlier, our first girl was born two days before the wife's. Only one man can plan that eight years apart. I went to the waiting room to bring her in to meet and be the first to hold the newest member of our family. I asked her if it was okay if she had a brother, and she looked at me like "Are you for real?" and then said "That's okay too, Dad." I told her to "come hold your new sister," and she jumped up smiling from ear to ear. I took her in to hold her sister, and as she held her, the smile never left her face, as if it was her own living doll. Our life was almost normal for the next few years with very little depression. I was focused on the job at hand.

The job I had for the last five and a half years was one where you were to achieve more or maintain each month's sales from the previous year, and I was succeeding in just that but that meant I worked every day and came in on my days off to achieve it. Still I wasn't getting the recognition I thought I deserved for trying to be "perfect" and pleasing everyone but myself. I began to spiral down, feeling unneeded the same feelings I hung on to all these years and I quit. I thought I wasn't good enough for my boss because he always glared at me with the same look that my dad gave me just before he would yell or smack me. I went into that "poor me" mode I had learned so well from my father. I just didn't know it then.

After a month without work and beating myself and my family up emotionally, I started my own company where I could create my own hours. It worked for a while until I was so busy in the second year I was back to being at work every day including Sundays. My emotions are up because I'm busy and down in the dumps when I'm not. My life was becoming what I now know as an emotional roller coaster, and it affected the family without me realizing it for the next twelve years.

I became more focused on the company and assumed my family would always understand that I'm doing this for them. What I wasn't focusing on now was hiding the childhood scars and horrible emotions, and those needed more control than what I had to give. They began coming to the surface after a violent attack resulted in a head injury in 2007.

My drinks got stronger as I tried to get the memories of that night I was beaten by a group of teens armed with skateboards off my mind. The attack came after they smashed the side glass on our vehicle, and as I jumped out, I told my wife to take the girls home (four twelve year old girls) and call the police. Here come my protecting and controlling qualities that I developed growing up.

Because they were kids, I only used force when I had to. I just tried to keep them away from me as I had never touched a kid before that day. Even pushing them away felt wrong, but I wanted justice for the damage to our vehicle and for the girls. I continued holding them off as I counted four with skateboards and five or six without. There were another eight to ten just watching as I tried to push them away each time they'd get close.

There was a girl and a guy getting my attention right in front of me, and I stopped looking around for a split second. I caught a flash out of my left eye. It was a distraction so the coward to my right could swing away, so I tried to move out of the way but—*crack*—I got violently spun around from a direct hit to the right side of my head. The hit was so hard that my ring came off my right hand and bounced with the slowest slow motion, high-definition *ting, ting, ting, ting* as I slowly lost consciousness.

The next memory I had was getting up to one knee, and they were all gone. I did notice one car still there, but with this horrible high pitched ringing in my ears, I was deaf to the two girls who stayed until I woke up. I started walking to the north as the girls were driving slowly beside me, trying to talk to me, and their lips were moving, but I just couldn't hear them till the ringing quit. I stumbled another few feet, looked up, and saw my wife come around the corner, and it was then that I heard the girls say, "Do you need an ambulance?" and one was there quickly. The girls said they hit me repeatedly in the head while I was out but not one body shot. They knew some of the kids but didn't want trouble from them and left.

And from that day forward, it has been an emotional night mare to say the least. A very large piece of my life will never be the same again. Now my mental health has declined a lot from not wanting to do anything and not going out even on beautiful days, from depression to aggression, up and down and up and down.

I'm frustrated at the justice system, and our health care couldn't help with my memory, and all I could smell was perfume for two of those years. My speech and writing skills lessened to the point of giving up the one thing I built up for fourteen years, and that was my company because I couldn't remember customers or what car they bought after just a day or two. Knowing I did have a great memory before the attack was hard to come to grips with.

Now I'm trying to get our health system to find why my symptoms are still with me and I was without medication for what I really needed and had painkillers that only worked on my headaches. I continued to have memory and speech problems, and the neurologist told me when the injury happened that these symptoms should diminish after one year. "Ya sure, Doc."

By then, I was going crazy with anger and rage issues and losing my mind as another year slipped by. Depression like I never had before hit in the third year with financial problems and more personal problems mounting from when the injury occurred. I just hit the lowest form of bottom that I could by putting my family through those last three years of yelling at any little thing. The depression worsened, and I was thinking that I would never get better. It was denial that kept stopping me from reaching out and asking for help as it kept sinking me deeper and deeper. I literally gave up on any doctor who couldn't see how stressed my life was.

My wife moved in with her parents because my moods were out of control. I was on my own then for the first time in twenty five years, and for the first month, I was lonely, mad, and frustrated all the time. It wasn't doing me any good thinking of suicide all the time. Now with depression thinking for me came more drinking, and I now know what recipe that was. It wasn't a delicious one. A hunting rifle is how I could do it the quick and easy way, but I would drink till I passed out first.

A lot happened, as well as a lot of crying out for help to my children with letters and texting the wrong words. A SWAT team met me one morning, but they told me they were there all night. I asked, "Why not bang on the window to wake me up like you did this morning? Because I would have come out just the way I did now and saved the taxpayers some money." His answer was

"Just following protocol," and when they heard it was me, some who knew me said I would come out right away. And I would have if I wasn't sound asleep in the basement, with no phones and the door closed and with the furnace running ten feet away. I didn't hear anything but the *bang, bang, bang* seven hours later.

Let's face facts. Nothing happens in Moose Jaw, and the rookies needed training. That was how I felt then, and of course I feel the same now, but being taken in did help me with the depression from all those horrible moods up and down and memory and speech issues. So for that, I'll never be more thankful.

It was then that I met with whom I'll call "the good doctor" with whom I shared my history with the head injury and why my symptoms are now so frustrating and how I was losing control from not having the answers to help my rage and depression. The next day, he ordered a full evaluation to be done immediately. I started my therapy early in 2010. It was a brain battle from then till March 3, with so many tests and studies of my capabilities. But at least I wasn't ignored anymore. Today I received the results.

I truly found out through the therapy and studies with the two ladies with the same first and last initials, JS. I'll say that these two JSs were making it very clear to me that my immediate memory was virtually gone, as I've been saying for the past three years. Some of the studies were done on my wife, using a rating system on what I could accomplish before the injury, and an in depth study was done on myself, with memory and speech testing that would some days make me angry to where I wanted to just give up but I couldn't now that the doctor had me thinking of hope.

I was given a prescription of different chemicals to slow the depression and control the aggression, hoping memory and speech would follow. I was finally beginning to "relax." I could see that there might be a light at the end of the tunnel. My speech was still messed up, but from that day on, I started to write anything bad I'd said or done that I could remember. I'm not proud of writing some things as you will read, but I wanted to use writing as my therapy with memory. I would write down anything to see if the words would come out right, and like my speech, they wouldn't.

I was driven now and I just kept on writing and reading it back over and over until it made sense. Then I trained myself to remember what I wrote repeatedly for months. In between this time, I didn't take my medication all the time because I felt somewhat better. That turned out to be a big mistake because I would say and do and write horrible things. Thinking back to when my wife left, it brought out emotions again. I was more abusive to myself to the point of suicide attempts, and it showed I wasn't good at that either. I left many letters behind, some good, loving, humorous, and meaningful just in case it happened. This one I wrote when I was still frustrated with speech and memory. I call this "Chasing Memories":

I remember that I remembered to do something that I had to do, but I can't remember what that might have been, and Just when I thought I had remembered to do it, I'm reminded that I still can't remember it at all. Then I remembered to remind myself to write a note of what I could remember and by the time I started I just lost it all together."

So when it all seems hopeless and lost, just remind yourself of the memories you can remember and not cling to those you don't. They say not to dwell, hanging onto negatives that I can't remember, but to focus on things I used to do very well like write, draw, or build things around the house, just to keep busy and remember the things I can.

So I did just that, and I tried and tried to write as I did before the injury. I kept pushing and pushing myself too hard, so I thought I would bring out a poem I wrote back on September 14, 2001, as the world was in shock as I was, to inspire my mind to write again. My shop was just being built back then, and I didn't have to be there much, so I wrote this sitting and thinking what kind of a world we live in. If our neighbor could be the enemy, how safe are we? I'll share it with you.

Face to Face:

We live in a secure and powerful place

Terrorists are amongst us face to face

They enter our country and plot for hours

As they plan their attack, on the mighty twin towers

Terrorists are amongst us face to face

Will we ever feel safe in this once,
secure and powerful place?

Now as we watch them remove and uncover

What once was buried and now we recover

The thousands of loved ones that perished

The New York skyline we all knew and cherished

It will be never the same to build another

So a monument should be for our fallen brother

And never again shall we suffer such an attack

As the government promised to pay them back

It will take a long time and many a tear

As we'll always be reminded of
September 11th each year

Terrorist are amongst us face to face

So let's all come together to make it safe

So we can live in this secure and powerful place.

Now it should be something I could remember repeating word for word, but I couldn't. Okay, I would keep writing it out over and over and over again just to remember my own words. So it's like school again, but I'm the teacher this time, and my goal was getting my sanity back but not before frustrating and torturing myself because it was taking too long. Now I wanted to just give up. It was easier and less painful to die, especially when there was so much depression following me everywhere I went.

I take the medication faithfully now but not before another attempt. Here is the letter I'm not proud of, but it got me the help I needed.

She left my heart broken and she never said goodbye.

The girls and I fought for counseling,
but she wouldn't even try.

Maybe twenty five years of love
was nothing but a lie.

There is surely some reason why she
couldn't look me in the eye.

It's just taking too long for the real reason why.

My mind is so confused thinking she
must have wanted me to die.

Girls:

Just Look up to heavens just beyond the sky.

Even as I enter my new world, I'll still be close By.

I'm all better now, there's now need to cry.

The clouds will soon leave me, as
I'm quickly soaring high.

Remember the happy times and
when I wasn't this bad guy.

I'll be in your hearts forever.
Be good to each other, for your
mother's sake please try.

I truly promise to watch over from heaven,
for it's here we cannot lie.

The rage is making me crazy and that's the real reason why.

In writing my story and for me to admit my past let alone let others read it is very hard, but it's my therapy to remember who I was, why I did or said hurtful things and who I am today. To find myself writing through so many of these emotions is truly hard. How I acted on them and why after the injury they came out in waves.

There is a positive to every negative.

Being alone "sucks." There are more things for me to do. I knew I could cook. I use the washer and the dryer less but have to clean out a messy flower garden and plant new flowers alone and use a weed whipper more but less dishes. I don't have to make a bed if I'm the only one in it, and I don't do windows. Vacuuming is a work in progress. I don't scream unless it's at myself; I can't pack a shed like she could, and doing it all lefthanded is tough because she has been my right hand for the past twenty five years. The only problem with a brain injury is remembering to do them without someone reminding me. So without my smartphone, I'd be lost these days.

If she hadn't left me, I believe I never would have met the doctor that requested the studies and counseling to find that after a life of no help, there was hope now and the medication to calm the aggression and the depression. I thought I would need more drugs than that just to stop the denial alone.

With me taking these meds, I can finally pay attention to what's been happening to my mental health, but when I heard the word "health," I associated that with things like my neck, my back, or my heart. So I'll stop the denial. It is mental, and it is my health and what I was really needing. I could never take time to do or think of mental health, let alone say it or relate it to me. I get it now and if I wasn't a workaholic, I would have had time like normal people to have holidays to release some stress. I'm not drinking now to feed my depression, and it becomes clear, yes, that I was stressed, but I made that stress with substance.

Whenever I made a breakthrough in my thinking, I would write many apologies for her to read one day like these next three.

I'm sorry I had you and the girls emotionally hijacked without knowing it for years, and it's hard for me to admit that, but I thought I was loving my family the only way I knew how to. I always loved you all and thought I was keeping everyone safe by keeping you near me, but I'm learning that it was a controlling behavior I learned early on in life.

I wrote this one a few months after.

I was stuck in my own sick and pathetic bubble,
So sorry I wasn't looking past
each and every double.

Since you took my left hand and became my wife,

You gave me reason to change my way of life.

I pray day and night I won't lose my soul mate.

The Lord brought us together through love and fate.

You are the glue that could bond many soles;

You are what I need to achieve all my goals.

I pray that you return each and every night.

I want you to be with me and for "that" I will fight.
My record's not great, but I can't afford to lose.

So put me in coach and then you can choose.

I'll do everything it takes to see that grin.

So I'm getting rid of the demons buried deep within.

These past months, I couldn't miss you more.

I'm pledging my love to you for all
the anger you heard before.

I'm working on the past to better our future,

But the pain is still horrible; it's like
no numbing before the suture.

I cry when I pray and mention your name.

Remembering how beautiful you
are, just isn't the same.

I miss the touch of your soft, soft skin;

I'm thinking of you always in that way.

I hope it's not a sin.

I hope I'm still your soul mate,
as you will forever be mine.

I'm sending you a kiss tonight and
imagining it tasting oh so fine.

Medication made me love myself again
and happier feelings are here.

So to all the young women in my
life, for this I am sincere.

My revelations "3:2 my 1"gee, I'm out numbered.

The medication I will take to my grave, without
missing a single pill, and this time, the words I'm saying I
truly mean because I'm finally understanding that trying
to control what I can't was wrong and the only thing I can
or will control is my actions and the way I react to them.
You have been my medication for far too long. No matter
what I've done in the past to achieve my goals in life and
try to find my calling, they are only objects, the same
as my trophies in business. I always tried for perfection
in whatever job I had, but the biggest achievement or
trophies I've truly accomplished was bringing both of
you girls into this world. When you were born, you gave
me a purpose to work my hardest at any job or trying to
play with you and your friends any minute I could spare
from working, with not a lot of family holidays because
of me trying to be perfect at work. I'm saying now I'm
sorry I didn't take more time in my life to realize my true
job was with you and how hard it was on you kids and
Mom. I know my mouth was loud, but I truly just wanted
to turn out two beautiful young ladies, and you both are
truly perfect. Your mother did a great job without me
being emotionally stable and thinking I was coping with
the family normally, if there is such a state of mind. I
love you all, and I thought I tried my best but my best is
yet to come.

The thing is I've been broken down as a child and carried depression without ever bringing memories to the surface for years, coupled with a head injury, which spelled trouble. I still continue to punish myself for my controlling issues, but trying to control things from childhood until now will take more of my "relax, release, reboot" method. But I have great support and tools to help me deal with all this now.

Letter to myself:

Life

Life will take me for granted if my life is uncontrolled.

Life takes life away not knowing who, when, or why.

When life takes a life from life, it is
sadness and memories that live.

If I take a life from life, it's hurt, anger,
and torment that live.

So before I'll take my life from life,

I remind myself that I'll never see, smell,
touch, taste, or hear someone say "I love you"
in this life again,

So if you want life to take your life,
it will but not before it's ready.

A renewed life is the only constant reminder of life.

So if you know someone suffering, then try to get them help because their life is important. Writing this was to make myself aware of how I can release my "problems" today as I wish I could have done then. I know what you're thinking! It's not my fault. But it just hit me that in life, we have many situations and how some of us turn them into problems. I'm realizing that our problems are the result of not addressing the immediate situation and just releasing it. A situation should be easy for anyone to deal with, only if you are not clouded by the things we are taught early on in life like our controlling behaviors, and that aggression rules because that makes it a problem when our mind is looking too far ahead of a small situation and it builds a bigger and bigger problem that can take years to release, as in my case.

Now to release you of life's problems more easily, first, be aware of one and, second, just think back to when it was a situation before you blew it out of proportion because that's when the situation can truly be solved quickly. "Oh, if I only knew of this then, it would have been a lot less to cope with now."

My brain is now rebooting and starting to give me a purpose and meaning in expressing what was locked up and was taking me down way too far and for far too long. And my key to the lock is found again, but I almost drowned in doing so.

So if you are having trouble believing in something good instead of self destruction, then it's time to find your "key" before you reach a dark bottom and they see you weak because your inner demons might not let you go this time. I was close and it's not a trip I plan on taking again. It's as if the Devil could make God bleed, and then we will seize to believe in his power and the devil in mankind will take advantage of the weak. I refuse to bleed emotionally again and then to see that happen in me. I blamed God for far too long and for too many things in my life, but I'm not going to be one of them anymore.

It has been months of treatment, counseling, and medication, and I have a long way to go memory wise, but I've always pushed myself to achieve my goals, and now my goal is simplified. My brain is the most incredibly important tool to process where I've been, where I go, and who I become. The best memory therapy was and is to write everything down *as my iPhone has been my memory through* It all. I will have to do this most likely for the rest of my life.

Oh, and I'm not angry at the kids who caused my injury, just sad for the memories they gave my twelveyearold daughter and her three friends. They were just walking to get snacks for a sleepover and were asked things that twelveyearold girls shouldn't have to be asked to do. So they ran to another store and called us to pick them up to confront the boys. Kids with sick minds and no respect for anything or anyone are getting away with whatever they want. Laws have to be changed, and Parents, it's called proper disciplining before they're out of control.

So it was a lot of effort to write this because if you knew me from 2007 up until early 2010, you would be amazed as I that I could have remembered to eat, let alone write again.

I tried different methods to "unwind" as I tried that "word" over and over. I learned that trying to unwind depression takes a long time and pain, and you just end up more wound up again and again. I look at a depressed brain as a tangled fishnet filled with hundreds of hooks, and the more I try to unwind it, the more tugging it takes and the hooks keep making new and deeper scars. Forget the word *unwind* because it's only used for ropes, cables, coils, wires, etc., not your mind. Do this; it works quicker and is less painful: relax release reboot.

It sounds more soothing, and you'll feel less pain and relax your thoughts. Don't tug on them. Relax the scars. There are no more hooks. You can now release the clutter and just unplug your mind, as now your reboot is finally starting.

It's hard to think that my own words helped me faster than anything else I've tried before. So as I put them into action, these emotions I held in my mind for years have been truly jumping out and on to paper faster than I've ever thought. If a mind like mine can be opened after being very badly buggered, then yours can too.

So in closing, I'd like to share with you this short note I wrote to myself that was not hard to write, but if you do it in your mind while trying to remember the words as slow as I wrote them, I guarantee they will relax you. I can't read it slowly any more than twice before I'm yawning, and if I start to close my eyes and say them, I will be almost asleep. Good luck.

I live and let love in my heart each day. I forgive myself but don't forget myself, and I'm giving myself precious time to breathe... and... breathe... and to slow down now... to see what I can do, to... really... really... really...really ... really... truly... truly relax... and to release... and breathe and release... release... to reboot. And when you can remember and say each word *slowly in your mind,* then that's great, but the truth is I think you'll be very relaxed before then.

I'm so glad today that I endured in sharing my life struggles on what triggered my depression, aggression, and drinking that turned my situations into big problems. But if my story can touch just one soul with undetected depression then I'm happy. But if it left you feeling guilty, angry, horrified, sorry, anxious, sick, bored, and hurt and/or it made you laugh or cry, then I'm truly sorry because that's the emotions and the courage it took for me to complete it.

Thank you for reading these words that my brain has finally released. I know there is more to tell you about my life *that will come later,* as this part of my life was the most important for me today. As in sales, I would always tell what needed to be repaired first before the purchase, so when they are fixed, you could enjoy all the good things for years to come.

I know I feel better. How about you

Pacific Book Review

helping authors succeed!

Title: Relax, Release, Reboot
Author: Kim Hoffman
Publisher: Great Writers Media
ISBN: 1956517057
Genre: Autobiography/Self-Help
Pages: 44
Reviewed by: Beth Adams

Pacific Book Review

It is said good advice, taken wisely, creates a man who learns from the mistakes and mishaps of others, therefore not having to repeat them in this own life. This autobiographical book is exactly the humble reveal of mostly many unfortunate events of Kim Hoffman. In his memoir titled *Relax, Release, Reboot*, the author peels away the fluff of daily events which had no significance on his life, yet expands quite humbly the most memorable, powerful, tragic, and revealing moments which have shaped the author's life.

Relax, Release, Reboot is a rather short read, allowing it to be easily completed in one sitting, forming what could be described as the genre of a story told in an Alcoholics Anonymous meeting. Yes, details highlighting many positive memories, such as raising pigeons in the attic, even capturing the birds on a train trestle were fun to read. The "love at first pinch" when he met his beautiful wife-to-be, and ultimately the mother of his two children was inspiring as showing fate has a defined role in life. Kim Hoffman's ambition and striving for perfection in his business successes shows a side of his personality which is very impressive. Yes, there is even some comic relief when he writes about a trip to Mexico, and being from Canada, burning up on the first day from the hot sun. Yet throughout, all readers are pulled down into the mental disorder, dysfunctional, often violent and truly sad life which he has lived. This is a book of redemption and provides readers a generous dose of self-help for those who may be afflicted by alcoholism, drugs, domestic violence and loneliness.

Kim Hoffman has written some poetry which he graciously showcases in this book. It shows a depth of emotional maturity and humanism of the author. Tragically, being struct in his head by a group of young teenagers with skateboards, falling unconscious from a blow to his head, has caused years of rehab and drug therapy, of which caused problems of its own. The take-away of his advice is the title: *Relax, Release, Reboot.* This advice, well presented to intelligent readers, may in fact be just what is needed to have others learn from the mistakes of Kim Hoffman; and if this occurs, then the goal the author has set out to achieve had been accomplished.